THE BOOK OF
TOTAL
SNOBBERY

THE BOOK OF TOTAL SNOBBERY

Lynne & Graham Jones

New English Library

Illustrated by Max Ellis

British Library Cataloguing in Publication Data

Jones, Lynne
   The book of total snobbery.
   1. England. Social class
   I. Title   II. Jones, Graham
   305.5'0942

   ISBN 0-450-48552-8

First published in Great Britain 1989

Published by New English Library,
a hardcover imprint of Hodder and Stoughton,
a division of Hodder and Stoughton Ltd,
Mill Road, Dunton Green, Sevenoaks, Kent TN13 2YA
Editorial Office: 47 Bedford Square, London WC1B 3DP

Photoset by Rowland Phototypesetting Ltd
Bury St Edmunds, Suffolk

Printed in Great Britain by
St Edmundsbury Press Ltd, Bury St Edmunds, Suffolk

Acknowledgements

The authors would like, first and foremost, to thank Bob Oxby for suggesting the basic idea which led to this high-minded volume during a meal break at the *Daily Telegraph*; also Mrs Annie Walker, late of the Rovers Return Inn, Weatherfield (after all, she was a Beaumont of Clitheroe) and our greatest, noblest, closest, and dearest friend, Cecil, 21st Duke of Cricklewood, (his good Grace, as we call him) without whose precious support, kindness, warmth, and inspiration, there would never have been a book at all.

We are also grateful to the publishers of all Britain's daily and Sunday national newspapers, plus *Harpers & Queen*, *Elle*, the *Tatler*, *Vogue*, and sundry other glossies for providing the basic raw material. We consulted some 200 books and the most productive sources, where not listed in the text, appear in a select bibliography. Anyone who feels he or she has been unjustly snubbed, omitted, or the victim of outrageous literary snobbery is invited to contact the publishers for inclusion in future editions of this assuredly most superior work.

Snobbery is the religion of England.
Frank Harris

It is impossible, in our condition of society, not to be sometimes a snob.
William Makepeace Thackeray,
The Book of Snobs

Contents

Introduction

You are obviously too much of a lady or a gentleman even to deign to think about it, but have you read the recent spate of articles in *Burberry and Bystander* yet? Yes, suddenly *snobbery* is back in vogue.

Only a handful of years ago it seemed that to become successful and admired you needed to read *Cloth Cap and Black Pudding Weekly*, drop your aitches, dress down for dinner, and plead poverty approaching the National Debt. Not any longer.

Today you cannot hope for social or career advancement without designer Wellingtons, holidays in Goa, Nepal or Rajasthan, a town house in Chelsea and membership of the New Young Fogeys club in Pall Mall. These days *anyone who is anyone* can spot a grey shoe, a clip-on bow tie or a fake Louis Vuitton bag at one hundred paces.

Despite being such an important social skill, snobbery as a subject has been treated rather condescendingly in the past, with the odd notable exception such as Thackeray or Nancy Mitford. This "new snob's bible" is an attempt to redress the balance. Rather like the argument over old money and new, this book looks at snobbish attitudes, old and new. The old go back to that grand, superior Greek, Socrates, through Thackeray, the man who put snobbism on the map, and the likes of the 11th Duke of Bedford who posted look-outs wherever estate workers toiled. The workers would then be made to dive out of sight whenever His Grace approached so that the ducal eyes were unsullied by observing menial labour.

But this book is rather more a guide to the new snobbery, and how it might be achieved by the uninitiated: the home gym and a CD player in the XJS for him, the Claude Montana two-piece for her; and for his or her pet, the very latest in designer Chum.

9

We give tricks-of-the-trade such as how to combat the property price bore (rent); how to meet royalty on the cheap (go to polo matches or scan the glossies for cut-price tickets to royal charity galas) and how really to impress the neighbours (buy a clapped-out old yacht, stick it on a trailer, and take it out to a car park on the coast).

It is said that a true snob never knows he or she is a snob, because what is snobbishness to the rest of the world is merely natural superiority to them.

We have to admit to a little home truth ourselves: no one who was *not* at least in part a snob could have penned this high-hatted tome. Put it all down to William Makepeace Thackeray, who with delightful characters such as General Scraper, Miss Snobky and Sir George Granby Tufto, KCB, KTS, KH, KSW, etc., etc. wrote the definitive *Book of Snobs* in 1846.

For it was here on page two of this serenely superior work that we were able to read the advice: "Smith or Jones, my fine fellow, this is all very well, but you ought to be at home writing your great work on SNOBS."

Mr Thackeray sub-signed his piece "By One of Themselves" and, having elbowed old Smith aside, we were for a time minded to call this great work on snobs: *How to Keep Up With the Joneses: By Two of Themselves.* But we naturally didn't want the poor man's work compared unfavourably with ours.

Royal dukes and *Burberry and Bystander* apart no one can read this book, we believe, without recognising a little of themselves and laughing along, we hope, with one of the great irreversible quirks of human nature.

Graham Jones
Lynne Jones
Hertfordshire, 1989

PART I
What is a Snob?

Drawing the Line

*I'm sure there is no greater snob than a snob
who thinks he can define a snob.*
Russell Lynes, *Snob*

Thackeray's definition of the beast changes through his *Book of
Snobs*, as its meaning has done in history itself. In the beginning,
he is a man or woman "who eats pease with his knife", but later
this becomes one "who meanly admires mean things" – a rather
sharper assessment.

Perhaps the most convenient definition we read was by Professor Norman Stone ("Stamp out this snob Society", *Mail on
Sunday*, August 1986). He boldly asserted that the word comes
from the Latin. *In Oxford, in the old days, you wrote s.nob. against your
name in the register of undergraduates if you were* sine nobilitate,
meaning without nobility. *These students looked up to their aristocratic
fellows and down on the people who were their own inferiors.*

Conventional theory has it that the word "snob" originally
meant a cobbler or shoemender and from thence it was an easy
step for it to be used to describe hoary-handed sons of toil in
general. But it was in Cambridge (not Oxford!) that it became
applied to "town" against "gown". It meant a particular
"Scullion"-type position in the social hierarchy and the way
persons of that rank (Warrant Officer II) were expected to behave
– fawning to their betters, always trying to assume a place higher
on the social ladder. From this the term came to be applied to one
who attached an unreal importance to accidents of birth, rank and
wealth.

Evelyn Waugh defined snobbery thus: – *the basic principle of
English social life is that* everyone *(everyone, that is to say who comes to
the front door)* thinks he is a gentleman. *(Unless she is a lady – Ed.).
There is a second principle of almost equal importance:* everyone draws
the line of demarcation immediately below his own heels.

Snobbery is actually endemic in the animal and bird world too (notably camels and, as Harold Nicolson pointed out, hens – no Edwina Currie jokes please). But it is also commonly (oh-so commonly!) assumed that aristocrats are at the forefront of the art, human-wise. Not so: it is overwhelmingly a middle and upper-middle class affectation as the combatants try to pitch their tent on the home estate of the truly blue-blooded.

We are very democratic here. Our committee consists of three ladies, three women and the village schoolmistress.
President of the Women's Institute, quoted by Flora Thompson, *Lark Rise to Candleford*

We have been careful in our book to separate snobbery and racial ill-feeling which is something quite different. It is true, however, that national jingoism reinforces snobbery: look at any English-speaking expatriate community where the rules and social pecking order are maintained far more fiercely than at home in the old country. It is also true that nations without much of an aristocracy become rather fawning about other people's. Nowhere was the tendency seen more clearly than among Hitler's Nazi high command. So obsessed were they with the British nobility that they set up a collection of POW notables at Colditz (the Earl of Harewood, Earl Haig, the Earl of Hopetoun and the Master of Elphinstone among them), then sent their second-in-command parachuting in to Scotland to meet the man they seemed to regard (though others didn't) the most important in Britain at the time, the Duke of Hamilton.

Nevertheless, while occasionally taking a nostalgic look at the magnificent snobberies of yore this is fundamentally a book about modern attitudes: of party precociousness and the dreaded opening phrases such as "When we were in the Maldives ...."; of fashion name-dropping "I wouldn't be seen dead without my Armani jacket . . ."; of food and wine snobbery and the here-today-gone-tomorrow cults such as Cajun cuisine.

Have we delineated snobbery for you? If not, it is probably wise to retreat to Thackeray: *The word snob,* he concluded, *has taken a place in our honest English vocabulary. We can't define it, perhaps. We can't say what it is any more than we can define wit, or humour, or humbug. But we know what it is . . .*

A World of Snobs?

I have been struck everywhere in England with the beauty of the higher classes. The nobility and the gentry differ from their peasantry as the racer differs from the dray-horse or the greyhound from the cur.

Nathaniel Parker Willis, US
journalist, 1834

I have been dragged along to this third-rate place for a third-rate dinner for third-rate people.

The late broadcaster, Gilbert
Harding, at an engagement in Hounslow,
1953. (In the uproar which followed he
was forced to leave.)

I hated being this "Cheery Janet" character on the Six O'Clock Show. It wasn't me at all. I don't shop down the street market and I'm not riveted by the price of bloody fish. I go to the opera. My friends are artists. I live in a big house.

Janet Street-Porter, Q Magazine

Oh yes! To adapt an Arab proverb – the dogs bark, but the caravan of snobbery continues. You don't believe us? Well let's, in the immortal words of Loyd Grossman, examine the evidence, in a number of important worlds:

Politics and Diplomacy

Remember the high-handed sneers at the "Cowboy President"? Well, he might have been adjudged a political success. But other heads of state found his folksy charm more difficult to accept. No smile could have been more forced than that of the Queen when she found herself compelled to ride alongside the hicksy horseman in Windsor Great Park.

Meanwhile the grand elitist himself, ex-President of France, Giscard d'Estaing, had these precise, cold and condescending words to say about Ronald Reagan after a forty minute tête-a-tête at the White House:

I find the President very informed about world problems, despite their being so complex.

★   ★   ★

Working-class Labour MPs still find themselves on the receiving end in that most un-gentlemanly of gentlemen's clubs, the House of Commons. Deputy leadership contender John Prescott has never been allowed to forget that he was once a Merchant Navy steward: the typical cry from the Tory benches when he rises to his feet is – "Two gin and tonics!" With the addendum from the portly and bellicose form of Nicholas Soames, grandson of Churchill, "And the same again for my friend over here, Giovanni."

★   ★   ★

That is not so say that Labour grandees are not without their own class hatred. Richard Crossman was spiteful about the working class element of the workers' party in his diaries on the subject of the investiture of the Prince of Wales in 1969 –

Thank God I am not Lord President of the Council any more concerned with all the flummery. It was the working-class members of the Cabinet who took part, Jim Callaghan and George Thomas, Harold Wilson, Michael Stewart and Fred Peart, and the Chief Whip, Bob Mellish would have been there if he had have been free. They could adore it and share in it but Barbara, Roy, Tony Crosland and I, the middle classes, are out of it.

Not that he could touch, in some people's view, the heights of former Labour deputy leader, later SDP luminary Roy (Lord) Jenkins as seen in his *Brussels Diary*: "their tediousness and self-importance were stupefying," wrote Charles Moore in *The Spectator*.

Thus Lord Jenkins drops the fact that a talk with the Pope was *much more intimate . . . than . . . with either of the other two Popes whom I have met.* He pronounces that King Baudouin of Belgium has a manner *quite unlike that of any member of the British Royal Family.* Talking of which, Prince Charles is (note the total lack of sycophancy) . . . *the most intelligent male member of his family since Prince Albert.*

"No doubt Lord Jenkins met him too," wrote Moore. Mind you, this was the man (Jenkins, not Moore) who said of James Callaghan: *You know: there is no case I can think of in history where a man combined such a powerful political personality with so little intelligence.*

★   ★   ★

We must not suggest that there is any less snobbery on the Tory Commons benches, of course. Speaker Bernard Wetherill is one who will readily testify to the chilly reception he, as a man in trade, was met with. There was horror when he confessed his background in gents' outfitting to a member of the old guard.

"Good God!" exclaimed one old buffer. "They're even letting tailors in now."

> *No one will ever know how many port and lemons I've downed in the interests of the Conservative Party – not real port, you know: the kind of port a publican may have.*
> Harold Macmillan, quoted by
> Peter Levi, the *Spectator*

The Aristocracy

While, as this book has been careful to point out, it is the middle classes rather than the men and women of "breeding" who are the real champions of snobbery, it must be acknowledged that the upper classes have a certain *élan* when it comes to shutting out the disagreeable, particularly when seeking the hands of daughters of noble birth in marriage.

One celebrated name much on the receiving end of doors slammed in his face was the poet, John Betjeman. It probably began at an early age when, at a children's party, he overheard a friend's mother (with due volume) refer to him as "a common little boy". And his rebuffs at the tongue of his prospective mother-in-law, Lady Chetwode, are legendary, though he did not endear himself by turning up to a white-tie dinner at the Savoy merrily twanging an imitation bow tie he had purchased to annoy his hosts.

Lady Chetwode was to refer to him as "that little middle-class Dutchman" and his friend Hugh Gaitskell's parents allegedly refused to ask him to their home because his father was "in trade".

Our favourite story of the nobility concerns, however, the family of the Duc de Levis-Mirepoix. Their title dated back to the ninth century of French aristocracy, though they plainly believed they had still grander connections. The story was that the family was descended from the sister of the Virgin Mary, and thus they began their nightly prayers, "Ave Maria, ma cousine . . ."

But other members of this elite group have made their feelings known on a variety of subjects:

Would Gruinard (anthrax-infected Scottish island) *once cleared not be a perfect permanent site for the hippies, who are having great difficulty in finding one? There are no farmers or neighbours to be upset. Pop concerts could be continuous and the hippies are less likely than other people to be bothered by any remaining germs.*
Lord Campbell of Croy in a House of Lords debate, 1988

Snobbery comes into almost everything one does. When my wife has a headache I know it is handed down from Mary, Queen of Scots. That gives a whole new element to migraine.
The late Sir Iain Moncrieffe of that Ilk, *Reveille*

Always be nice with young girls, one never knows whom they might not marry.
Lady Ailesbury, nineteenth century

Don't tell me you're going to the lavatory. It's too common, darling.
Lady Diana Cooper

During the season debs don't work. They work hard enough writing their thank you letters to their hostesses of the night before.
Deb's mother, 1957, quoted by Margaret Pringle, *Dance Little Ladies*

Transport

We all lament, of course, the demise of third class on British railways which naturally created more problems than it solved. One of the two authors was travelling to the country, and, dressed to match, entered her appointed compartment to meet a rather cantankerous grande dame who straightway challenged:

"Do you realise this is First Class?"

The reply was devastating: "Yes, of course. And do you realise you are sitting in my reserved seat?"

But our favourite story concerns the ticket office at Leamington Spa, which had the seeming eccentricity of making out third-class seasons to London to, say, Mr J. Smith while first-class seasons were made out instead to J. Smith, Esq.

This, decided regular travellers, smacked of inverse class distinction, but when challenged, the station master had the perfect explanation:

"You see the third-class holders travel to work six days a week but the first-class passengers only go up four or five times a week. Both seasons used to be Mr J. Smith but the wives of the first-class holders were using their husbands' tickets by changing Mr to Mrs in pencil, so we gently stopped their little game by changing to Esq."

Snobby it may sound but there's something about a Tube line which can drag an area down. It doesn't just make it easier for the residents to get out, it makes it easier for the rubbish to get in.

Sutton Herald, quoted by "This England", *New Statesman*

Finally, *Today* newspaper in February 1989 told the sad story of how the Duchess of York had won air tickets to Jamaica in a raffle, and had thoughtfully presented them to one of her staff and his lady wife. Explaining why she was not entirely happy with this situation, the wife explained:

The air tickets are tourist and we always fly first class.

Education

Since it seems eminently reasonable to the authors that anyone so minded should be entitled to pawn away much of the family earnings to secure Jones Junior a decent start in life, plus the odd ritual flogging to calm him or her down for the holidays, we shall not dwell unduly on the one-upmanship behind offloading one's sprogs at public and prep school.

However, two stories show how normal middle class common sense can give way to ostentation or insularity:

First, *The Times* told how five-month-old Master "X" was enrolled for St Aubyn's (*where* ?) after his father found himself seated next to the headmaster on an airline flight. And worse: the captain was apparently called as a witness.

Secondly, we were amused to read a pre-Big Bang story about the extent of the old school tie network in the city, centring on how Lazard Freres & Co. had managed to avoid making bad loans in the turmoil of the early 1970s which led so many firms to crash. Lord Poole, chairman of the firm, told Lord Cowdray, whose family owned the business:

"Quite simple: I only lent money to people who had been to Eton."

Recreational pursuits

There is a real chance for the master, or mistress snob to shine if he or she is invited to submit for publication a description of the mouth-wateringly superior people, places and events which make up his or her spare time.

The Sunday supplements go in for it quite a lot: "Who's Having Who for Sunday lunch", and a "Life in the Day of X". Our nomination for the best is the princess of the florid pen, Candia McWilliam, for listing in the *Telegraph* magazine (if *Private Eye* is to be believed): "pleasures of life" which included "singing bits of oratorio in empty train carriages"; "programming her dreams"; "reading Villiers de L'Isle Adam while eating a pomelo"; "the colours and trim of a pile of turnips"; Kingsley Amis; and cooking which she described instead as "beating against the tide in a homely coracle powered by well-deployed spoons".

The genre has been well set by lists of recreations in *Who's Who*. And our winner here is the theatre critic, Sir Harold Hobson, for "recollecting in regretful tranquillity the magical things and people I may never see again." There followed a six-line list of famous faces and places including Proust's Grand Hotel at Balbec, Sunday afternoon teas at the Ritz, the theatrical bookshop in St Germain-des-Prés, Madeleine Renaud and Jean-Louis Barrault.

> *A lot of the wrong sort of people are playing*
> *backgammon nowadays.*
> Suzy, US gossip columnist

> *The company's book,* Sellocraft, *is a little*
> *mine of items that children can make for*
> *themselves and for each other using normal*
> *household items (like champagne corks).*
> *The Times*, quoted by "This England",
> *New Statesman*

Royal Snobbery

*I have got a better background than anyone else
who's married into the Royal Family since the
war, excepting Prince Philip.*
Princess Michael

Since their acquaintance is, to many, the very height of social
ambition ("I danced with a man, who'd danced with a girl, who'd
danced with the Prince of Wales") it may come as a surprise – and,
to many of us, a delight – to discover that snobbish traits may even
reach the highest in the land: the Royal Family itself.

Thackeray traced the tradition: James I was not just a snob, but a
Scottish snob *and the world contains no more offensive creature.*
Charles II, his grandson, was a rogue, though not a snob: while
Louis XIV, *his old squaretoes of a contemporary, – the great worshipper
of Bigwiggery – has always struck me as a most undoubted and Royal
snob.*

If one Royal stands head and shoulders above the rest for her
grand successes in snobbery, it must be Princess Michael of Kent,
the glamorous Austrian-born divorcée whose impending arrival
enunciated the classic remark from the Queen herself: "She
sounds much too grand for us." And Viscount Linley, when asked
to nominate a gift for his worst enemy, declared: "Dinner with
Princess Michael."

Her stated ambition "to make the cover of *Horse and Hound* in
my own right" was said to sit ill at odds with the Royal ethos. She
didn't make *Horse and Hound*, but she did make *Wogan*, where she
told how she wanted to shoot the Queen's corgis.

Also a member of the public told this story of how the princess
had rung the Marquess of Bath to ask if she could bring her father
and stepmother to tea at Longleat; she had added "we don't want
any publicity", so the marquess told her to enter by the side door.

We don't tell stories of that sort.
The Princess of Wales to a joke-telling Duchess of
York, quoted by the *Evening Standard.*

25

The Bath contingent had just reached the coffee and brandy stage when they heard a din from the Great Hall. It was Marie-Christine sweeping in through the front door, pushing aside the tourists, generally doing the Royal bit, which was rather wasted, since no one knew who she was anyway.

The baron, his wife and Marie-Christine were then taken on a tour of the house. Seeing a lot of eager women tourists admiring a particularly beautiful room, Marie-Christine was heard to utter: "Ah, the peasants . . . why don't you tread on them?"

Mind you, it is sometimes difficult to keep up the highest of standards. When shortly before the birth of her first baby "Fergie", the Duchess of York, acquired a brown and white puppy called Bendicks, Royal watchers speculated on the breed. It looked a bit like a Jack Russell but there was just a hint . . . Surely a royal duchess wouldn't have a mongrel. Buckingham Palace

My favourite programme is Mrs Dale's Diary.
I try never to miss it because it is the only way of knowing what goes on in a middle-class family.
Queen Elizabeth, The Queen Mother, *Evening News*, quoted by "This England", *New Statesman*

solved that one by declaring the dog a Warwickshire Terrier. The Kennel Club said that they had never heard of such a breed.

And the ancient aristocratic lines of Europe do not necessarily regard the likes of Prince Philip as top drawer. Robert Lacey told the story of the English earl who asked his butler, after the Duke of Edinburgh had visited for a shooting weekend, what he had thought of the royal visit.

It had gone off "very well indeed, milord", replied the servant. "But he's a bit *nouveau*, don't you think?"

★   ★   ★

And finally . . .

The World's Greatest Snob

Mrs Ronnie Greville, the fearsome grand hostess of the 1930s, can rightly claim her place at the very top of the snobbery league, with not one but *two* of the haughtiest and most condescending quotes of all time attributed to her, viz:

"One uses up so many red carpets in a season."

And *"You mustn't think that I dislike little Lady Cunard – I'm always telling Queen Mary that she isn't half as bad as she is painted."*

Her success in climbing the social ladder is a legend. The illegitimate daughter of a Scottish brewer, she managed to ingratiate herself with virtually all the crowned heads and world leaders of Europe, and beyond, such as King Faud of Egypt. Among intimates were the King and Queen of Italy, the Queen of Spain, the Grand Duke and Duchess of Hesse and when Mrs G. declared:

"Three kings happened to be sitting on the edge of my bed this morning," she was telling the truth.

The key to her remarkable social success was her late husband, the Honourable Ronald Greville, who had been a friend of Edward VII and more importantly the husband of his mistress, Mrs Keppel. Thus she became as an intimate of the Duke and Duchess of York, to suffer a noble promotion on the abdication of Edward VIII. It was an entrée which allowed her complete freedom to put down her rivals, like Lady Cunard, and afforded her privileges granted to few other mortals. When for example, she declared herself unfit to attend Royal Ascot, the King and

Queen made available their private entrance. The thought of this had a dramatic healing effect and she was able to attend after all.

Abroad, Mrs Greville expected anywhere she visited to have a private train placed at her disposal. If it were not, the British ambassador would be sure to receive a reprimand.

Her poison was legendary. Harold Nicolson called her "a fat slug filled with venom", though in this she could be amusing as well as derogatory:

"To hear Alice Keppel talk about her escape from France, one would think she had swum the Channel with her maid between her teeth", and Lady Cunard was dismissed as *the lollipop*, a reference to Sir Thomas Beecham's collective name for lowbrow classics.

Her ostentation extended to bedecking herself from head to toe with the most enormous diamonds, which, because she was noticeably short, led her to being compared with a Christmas tree. She was never outdone in the jewellery department. When rival hostess Mrs Arthur James turned up at a ball showing four rows of pearls to her three, Mrs Greville was able to dig down deep into her bosom and produce another three rows, making a total of six.

Nor was she easily fazed: her two butlers, Bacon and Boles, were known for being habitually drunk while serving, and prone to helping themselves to the guests' fare, but she treated them as honoured family treasures. On one occasion one of the two was more inebriated at dinner than usual, and Mrs Greville scribbled him a note reading: "You're drunk. Leave the room at once." Bacon (or was it Boles?) with great presence of mind fetched a silver salver, put the card thereon, and presented it with a flourish to an astonished Mr Austen Chamberlain. He looked, looked again, put his monocle to his eye to check what he had read and finished the meal in a state of shocked silence.

During the war (which she naturally found quite tiresome) Mrs Greville took a suite in the Dorchester hotel where some sort of life was allowed to go on, as if Hitler failed to exist. There she was able to hold informal little gatherings that would include a few friends – say, the Mountbattens, the Duke and Duchess of Kent, the Duchess of Buccleuch, Prince Philip of Greece and Chips Channon. But she was now old and frail and four months after her last "royal" party in 1942, she died in her suite.

Even in death, though, Mrs Greville's superiority lived on. Her memorial service was the grandest of the war years with six

ambassadors, the archdukes of Austria and what was described as "half the nobility of England" in attendance. Perhaps her last and greatest triumph was however her £1,500,000 will.

This included the bequest of all her jewellery "with my loving thoughts" to the Queen. The famed Greville jewels, including the magnificent diamond necklace which had once been owned by Marie Antoinette, continued to be worn by Queen Elizabeth, the Queen Mother, at social and state occasions into her eighties. Who else but Mrs Greville could have arranged for a queen to wear her cast-offs?

An Important Warning – Things Can Backfire

*I know of no art, profession, or work for women
more taxing in mental resources than being a
leader of society.*

Mrs August Belmont, turn-of-the-century
Fifth Avenue hostess

She meant it, of course. All acts of grandeur and ostentation, that peculiar pleasure of putting down a neighbour, the sheer delight of possessions and experiences others can only aspire to, all must carry an official warning: snobbery can damage your health.

Witness Laura Corrigan, the wife of an American steel magnate, who arriving in London in 1921 by way of Cleveland, Ohio, New York, and Paris (where she had a château) was, within two years, giving the most lavish and talked-about parties in the capital.

The *Sunday Express* gossip column, which pursued and ridiculed her relentlessly, remarked:

When she comes back from the Sahara, I expect to find her sitting between two pyramids. After all, pyramids were made to climb.

(The paper also cruelly named her "Big wig of London" after her penchant for exotic artificial hairpieces, not quite in vogue in those days.)

But it was for her unfortunate social gaffes that Mrs Corrigan will largely be remembered.

W. G. Moore said to her: "*I always think, Mrs Corrigan, that of all the sexual perversions, chastity is the most incomprehensible.*"

Bemused she replied: "*I guess I shall have to think that one over, Mr Moore.*"

*　　*　　*

Introduced to Sir John Gielgud backstage after a production of *Hamlet*, she could think of nothing other than the fact that Hamlet was a Danish prince.

"*Why, I know the Danish royal family* intimately," she enthused.

*　　*　　*

Negotiating to rent the magnificent house at 16 Grosvenor Street

31

owned by Mrs Keppel, Edward VII's friend, she was told the Persian carpets needed to be treated with respect.

"*Why, they're not even new!*" Mrs C. exclaimed.

*   *   *

Her most glorious own goal came, however, when she had just returned to London from a Mediterranean cruise and David Herbert asked her:

"*Did you see the Dardanelles?*"

"*Oh, my, no,*" she said. "*But I did have a letter of introduction to them.*"

*   *   *

She was no intellectual, that is to be sure, a defect cemented in the public imagination for all time when she sent a card to George Bernard Shaw proclaiming: Mrs Corrigan, At Home, 6–8 p.m. Straightaway he returned the card with a scribbled message on the back reading: G.B.S. – Ditto.

The great bearded man of letters was always something of an elusive catch for the eager society hostess. Another of the upwardly clambering variety, Lady Sibyl Colefax (it was said that the only sound that could be heard in the blackout during the war was that of Lady Colefax climbing the social ladder) had a similarly distressing experience. Having told her maid to invite Mr B. Shaw to an intellectual evening she had arranged, she found herself face to face with Bobbie Shaw, the effete homosexual son of Lady Astor by a previous marriage.

"Can't imagine why they invited *me*," he murmured, finding himself completely out of synchronisation with the rest of the guests.

Though perhaps her greatest put-down came when the teasing Lord Berners invited her to a meal to meet the P of W. She eagerly jettisoned all other engagements in her diary only to find herself at the dining table next to the Provost of Worcester. Berners told her:

"*But Sibyl, I assumed you would be delighted to meet an estimable clergyman. I didn't think you were a social snob.*"

*   *   *

Another leading hostess to come to grief was Maud, Lady Cunard, who found that despite paying the necessary calls to her country neighbours at Nevill Holt, they did not seem to take to her. It might have been those little signs of ostentation she showed, like the huge ornamental gate constructed in her honour with the wrought-iron message: "Come into the Garden, Maud"; or the day she decided a particularly fine room, panelled in Tudor oak, needed brightening up. She ordered her servants to cover the oak with white gloss.

However, it was a particularly old local eccentric, Lord Mexborough, who was left to sum up local feeling: wheeled into the drawing room wearing a top hat, the noble lord shouted as soon as he saw her: "Take her away! Take her away!"

*   *   *

Sydney Smith had a devastating response to a posturing squire with whom he was out riding. Said the squire:

"If I had a son who were an idiot, I'd make him a parson."

Replied Smith: *"Quite so, though I see your father was of a different mind."*

*   *   *

Frank Harris, of *Life and Loves* fame, had a silver tongue and a grandiloquent manner. Nothing pleased him more than boasting of his social success, and the great houses where he had dined – until he met his match in Oscar Wilde:

"Yes, dear Frank, we believe you – you have dined in every house in London – once."

*   *   *

Another favourite put-down of ours concerns the scholar C. S. Lewis, whose slightly bedraggled appearance when entering the first-class carriage of a train somewhat startled an elderly lady.

"Have you a first-class ticket?" she inquired loudly.

"Yes, madam," said Lewis. *"But I'm afraid I'll be needing it for myself."*

*   *   *

An old club bore spent some time bending the ear of the great actor Sir Herbert Beerbohm Tree, and among copious reminiscences confided:

"When I joined this club, all the members were gentlemen."

"I wonder why they left," replied Tree.

*   *   *

Remembering how Nancy Mitford had chastised him for the use of the word "mirror" (it should have been "looking glass"), Sir Iain Moncrieffe of that Ilk challenged her on how he should describe to his sons an ancestor, beheaded in 1469, who was known as the Mirror of Chivalry.

She sent back a postcard: *Did they really call him that? How vulgar of them.*

★ ★ ★

Finally, in April, 1981, *Emmanuelle* star Sylvia Kristel was presented to the Queen Mother at a line-up at the Odeon cinema, Leicester Square.

"*Would you like to meet my director?*" she gushed, pointing to the man behind *Lady Chatterley's Lover*, Frenchman Just Jaeckin, poised ready in the row.

"*No thank you,*" replied HM crisply, as she moved on.

★ ★ ★

PART II
How to be a Snob

The New Snobbery

*The essence of snobbery is to arrange your life
in such a way that you must be considered a
person of importance if you know so many
important people; that you know such people
must be an observable fact, or it is wasted.*

Brian Masters, *Great Hostesses*

An interesting pointer to the aspirations of the new upper-middle class came in an article in *Harpers & Queen* in May, 1988, which surveyed the high points of which the new rich of Britain dreamed. Top fantasy was, apparently, sitting next to fashion designer, Jasper Conran, over a lunch of steamed brill while dressed in a Valentino cocktail dress, all the while making rude remarks about a businessman called Mr Ernest Saunders, who emerged as the least popular dinner party companion.

Half of *Harpers'* readers gave a dinner party once a fortnight, never in the kitchen, though few employed a cook. Ten per cent ate out in restaurants more than eight times a week. The most popular holidays were sunbathing in the Virgin Islands, safariing in Kenya, sightseeing in Rajasthan and skiing in Val d'Isère. The average spent on clothes was £3000 a year, with £6000 common.

Perhaps the greatest style-setter was the Kensington reader who indicated she spent £6000 a year on Armani jackets, never went to a dinner party, made love two hundred times a year and was more interested in resurfacing her tennis court than paying for a private

education for her daughter.

The following pages examine some of the areas in which the "new" is replacing the "old".

> *I'm not a snob. Ask anybody. Well . . .*
> *anybody who matters.*
> Simon Le Bon, *Woman*

The Right Way With Words

An Englishman's way of speech absolutely
classifies him. The moment he talks he makes
another Englishman despise him.

George Bernard Shaw

All the etiquette books will tell you: you cannot be a snob without correct mastery, not only of the English language, but of its pronunciation.

For the new snob, an accent is not so much important as its execution. In other words, it would be folly to try to ape an Oxford (upper class) accent if your vowels are pure Bolton. Best to go for the clipped military style of full frontal verbal attack; forget the gs, as in shootin', fishin', fornicatin'. Add lots of whats to the end of your sentences, following up with some *sotto voce* arp arps, as if a rather cross sea-lion. Talk *extremely loudly* at all times as if trying to get a gunman in the adjacent drawing room/railway carriage/country estate to give himself up.

The trick is to wax extremely lyrical about mundane, everyday happenings while retaining a detached interest about anything truly momentous. Hence a dash of wine spilt on the carpet, a clash of dresses, a bad word from a friend should be described as "absolutely awful", "frightful", "horrid" or "beastly". They are enough to make one "absolutely livid". The death of a loved one, a leg amputation or the loss of a country estate through gambling should correspondingly evoke no more emotion than a "bit of bad luck, that, eh?" and an instantaneous change of subject.

Naturally accents tend to change, chameleon-like, according to one's audience (just eavesdrop on any of your friends on the phone). One should try to maintain a standard; but at the same time remember that titles have to change according to prevailing circumstances. Thus a wife will address her husband as Mr

---

I would rather bite my tongue off than raise my
glass and utter the word "cheers"
John, Duke of Bedford, *Daily Sketch*, 1965

---

fforbes-Smyth in front of workmen, Harry in front of friends, and my husband in front of MFH or the vicar.

Rather a lot of nonsense was begun by Miss Nancy Mitford, who in 1956 wrote an article for *Encounter*, later expanded to a book, *Noblesse Oblige*, in which she included the views of one Professor Alan C. Ross on the correct usage of words to delineate one's social class. This was the famous U (for upper-class) and non-U, and England being the land of snobs it is, the official list caused a sensation.

Professor Ross classified the verb to commence as strictly non-U (U = to begin) but in *Hons and Rebels* Miss Mitford's sister Jessica revealed how they had called the family's favourite game "Hure, Hare, Hure Commencement."

Twenty expressions a true snob would never use:
   barnet (for hair)
   bonking (for engaging in sexual intercourse)
   ciao (for goodbye)
   crash (for finding sleeping accommodation)
   crumpet (for young lady)
   dog and bone (telephone apparatus)
   er indoors
   goinfurraspin (talking the motor car out for a run)
   gotcha
   hopping the pond (for flying across the Atlantic Ocean)
   innit?
   jamjar (for motor car)
   karzi (for lavatory)
   legless
   no sweat (never mind)
   rapping (for engaging in conversation)
   shampoo (for champagne)
   strides (flannels)
   watcha
   watsisname

And would we ever have remotely considered using the non-U "serviette" for napkin, "dentures" for false teeth, "dress-suit" for dinner-jacket, "sponge" for sponge cake, "corsets" for stays or "sweet" for pudding? You might as well have expected us to use a *cruet!*

The whole point of the exercise seemed to be that upper class people said lavatory, while the plebeians went to the toilet. Clearly Professor Ross thought ill (sorry, that's non-U, we mean sick) of what he had started and retired to the anonymity of Birmingham University to write a book about the less controversial Pitcairn Islanders.

To save your embarrassment, here are some pronunciations which you must master to join the new elite:

Abergavenny	– Abergenny, not Aber-guv-enny
Ate	– et, not eight
Balliol	– Bale-eol
Baulk	– Bork, not bollk.
Belvoir	– Beever
Brochure	– Broch-a, not bro-shure
Buccleuch	– Bu-clue.
Caius	– Keys.
Cherwell	– Char-well, not Chur-well.
Cholmondeley	– Chumley
Clique	– Cleek, not click.
Coronary	– Korenri, not kor-ron-eri
Derby	– Darby, not durby.
Economic	– Eek-onomic, not eck-onomic
Executive	– Egzeketif, not egzek-you-tif
Fault	– Fourlt, not falt
Forehead	– Forrid, not four-head
Garage	– to rhyme with barrage, not ger-arge.
Golf	– goff

The manager looked into the office adjoining his own and said: "I'm just off to lunch with the directors. You can go and have your dinner."
Quoted in Peterborough, *Daily Telegraph*, 1981

Handkerchief	– Hanka-chiff, not hanka-cheef or hand-cur-cheef
Harass	– Ha-rass, not harrus
Lamentable	– Lamment-abl, not lam-mentabl
Magdalen	– Mordlin
Marjoribanks	– Marshbanks
Marlborough	– Mawlboro
Marylebone	– Marry l'bun
Medicine	– Medsun, not med-i-sin
Norwich	– Norridge, not Noritch
Often	– offen, not oft-ten
Ralph	– Rafe not Ralff or Rorlf
Ruthven	– Rivven
Seymour	– Semer
Spinach	– Spinnidge, not spin-itch
Tortoise	– tort-us, not tort-oys
Vase	– Vars, not vays (we have vase of making you talk.)

Everyone I meet talks about "writing paper".
Notepaper is just not in the language.
Duke of Devonshire, *Sunday Telegraph* magazine,
1978

Intellectual and Artistic Snobbery

A certain amount of judicious snobbery is quite a good thing, besides being amusing.
A. L. Rowse

Whether by accident or design, in February, 1988, *Sunday Telegraph* writer and sociologist, Graham Turner, managed to produce the best ever anthology of intellectual snobbery simply by going to a glittering array of academic and artistic luminaries and asking them the question: "What do you think of the prime minister?"

Poet, Peter Porter thought her "bullying, stupid, and brutal". Designer, David Gentleman, called her "astonishingly paranoid, arrogant, tasteless and vain", and Alan Bennett said she was "a paid-up Philistine – typical of the people who go to the Chichester Festival".

Sir Peter Hall, director of the National Theatre, postulated that well over ninety per cent of people in education, the performing arts and the creative world were against her. Peter Nichols opined that she spoke for a new group of rising, working-class Tories. "The taxi drivers", he called them.

Jonathan Miller found her "loathsome, repulsive in every way". Hearing her talk, he said, was "like fingernails being drawn across a blackboard". It was "her odious suburban gentility and sentimental, saccharine patriotism, catering to the worst elements of commuter idiocy".

> *Tea-time walk-around talk-around in Soho to give ordinary people a chance of meeting me. I must admit I find the friendliness and informality of ordinary people quite delightful, even though some of them, I believe, are terribly poor.*
> Auberon Waugh, *Private Eye*

Mr Turner's article read not so much as a diatribe against Mrs Thatcher but a celebration of Britain's intellectual snob culture. Baroness Warnock, Mistress of Girton, denounced her as the worst of the lower middle class "packaged together in a way that's not exactly vulgar, just *low*".

This all explains why the Oxford dons refused her an honorary doctorate. But it underlines that when it comes to the snobbery of elitism, you can't beat an academic.

They may hone their barbs with a smile on their faces, of course. No one could accuse Dr A. L. Rowse, Emeritus Fellow of All Souls, historian, Shakespearean, and poet, of being anything but a nice old bean, but his pronouncements over the years have set new standards of *hauteur* and contempt for the common man. "I have genius," being a typical remark, "ordinary human beings are bloody idiots" being another.

With more than fifty books behind him and a bewitching, if at times aesthetic manner, Dr Rowse finds himself in constant demand for American chat shows, Ronald Reagan, not you might think an intellectual alter ego, having thanked him for inspiration in how to deal with Congress.

Dr Rowse shrugs all this off with typical conceit.

There's the paradox, dear, he told *The Times, not only am I absolutely first-rate, I am an enormous best-seller as well.*

The new snob might try to match these gems of intellectual snobbery (but remember Dr Rowse can at least back them up):

I don't live my life among ordinary human fools. I really am the most colossal highbrow, my dear. I'm hardly human, you know.

My real mission in life is to teach clods to use their brains.

I'm really rather fortified by my contempt for contemporary society. I'm happy working creatively for myself, I'm not interested in what third-raters think of them.

> *The truth is that ordinary people are incapable of working without direction.*

> *You cannot pigeonhole genius.*

And, perhaps to make the more egalitarian feel better:

> *I'm incorrigible, but then a lot of my conversation is in inverted commas. People don't see that. It's a joke, dear. You should see that. But these filthy fools don't, and so they are provoked. I've always been addicted to practical joking, but now it's taken a verbal turn.*

Some of the greats of literature were certainly snobs. The recently published first volume of T. S. Eliot's letters showed what a literary world climber he was. When Arnold Bennett joined Eliot's circle at a Bloomsbury party, Eliot left for another part of the room, bristling at Bennett's "lower middle class cockney accent". He asked his brother to secure him an introduction to the *Atlantic* with the recycled advice that: *Pound considers it important, wherever possible, to secure introductions to editors from people of better social position than themselves.*

Three more victims of intellectual snobbery were:

HAROLD HOBSON who as a youth went to interview the great George Bernard Shaw. Minutes into the interview, G.B.S. interrupted him and roared:

"Young man, have you come all the way from London to ask me these stupid questions?"

When Hobson said that he had, Shaw told him: *"Then you had better go straight back again."*

* * *

NANCY MITFORD who was not only declared non-U by the literary establishment for her famous article in *Encounter* about U and non-U, but who received this cruel put-down from Dame Edith Evans when told that she had been lent a villa so she could finish a book:

"Oh really? *What exactly is she reading."*

* * *

CHRISTOPHER HITCHENS, political journalist, who once filed a story about an event in Florence from Milan. After the predictable inquiry by his publishers, Hitchens answered that he thought Milan sounded more left-wing.

* * *

Artistic snobbery – particularly surrounding opera and ballet – is legendary. The story which perhaps best illustrates the opera world's penchant for preciousness is that of poor old Sir Rudolf Bing, of Glyndebourne, Edinburgh, and latterly of the Metropolitan Opera, New York. He was mugged in Central Park, losing his money and his watch. It was worth only some twenty-five dollars, but to Bing its being a British army watch and a souvenir of World War II, it was a favourite heirloom. The felony was naturally picked up by the New York newspapers.

You may have thought that his operatic colleagues might have had some sympathy. Not so. He received a severe reprimand from soprano Zinka Milanov:

"The general manager of the Metropolitan Opera does not carry a watch worth only twenty-five dollars," she fumed.

* * *

One of the best examples of artistic snobbery comes from the grand open-air concerts at Kenwood, and more specifically, Glyndebourne ("where even the peonies have swollen heads" – Anon). Here the two great snob cultures clash head on. On the

one hand, the ostentatious, champagne and caviar-downing for all to see; on the other, the music snobs who would gladly machete to death the artistic morons who applaud between the arias and even set up cameras on tripods, God forbid.

Clashes at a less prestigious, but equally strife-torn, event in Twickenham brought a letter to the *Richmond and Twickehnam Times* fuming that to keep the rabble out, surely the best solution was to allow into the enclosure only people bearing expensive wine – not cheap Australian Chardonnay or Fosters.

*   *   *

And other favourite Glyndebourne comments overheard include:

– The place is full of Eurobond dealers.
– Nonsense. They're double glazing salesmen.

He slept all the way to the interval, scoffed his champagne, and then went to sleep for the rest of the performance.

They converse in the interval with the most desolate ignorance.

Be early so your chauffeur can park the Rolls.

My dear, last year a fieldmouse *scampered across our picnic; we were sitting on a* nest. *The perils of Glyndebourne!*

*   *   *

There's not the quality of audience today. The stalls should be in dinner jackets or tails, and they're in singlets and bomber jackets. Quite awful! They come from places like Milton Keynes . . .
Sir Michael Hordern, *Sunday Express* magazine

But sometimes attempts at intellectual snobbery don't quite come off . . .

> *– Would you ever invite to your party people who weren't "society" but stars from another world – Luciano Pavarotti, say?*
> *– Oh, you wouldn't ask a* dancer. *I mean, he can contribute nothing. All he can do is dance.*
>
> Margaret, Duchess of Argyll, *Sunday Express* magazine (yes, we know Pavarotti dancing would be quite something.)

> *Graham Greene? But he's just a* writer, *isn't he?*
> Margaret, Duchess of Argyll, again.

> *I'm not talking about Tom Sharpe or David Lodge. I'm talking about Shakespeare. That's the kind of writer I should be compared with.*
> Howard Jacobson, interviewed by *Cherwell*

But let us not forget that however much we enjoy the jewel-encrusted sabres of intellectual snobbery, some other poor soul is inevitably on the receiving end:

> Jane Austen: *To me, Poe's prose is unreadable – like Jane Austen's. No, there is a difference. I would read his prose on a salary, but not Jane's.*
> Mark Twain

> Honoré de Balzac: *Can write the end of his book before he has finished the first paragraph, because he has turned all his creatures into clockwork cabbages and can rely on their staying put . . .*
> Samuel Beckett

48

Bertolt Brecht: *Brecht has not only never had an original thought, he takes twice as long as the average playgoer to have any thought at all.*
Robert Morley

Truman Capote: *A Republican housewife from Kansas with all the prejudices.*
Gore Vidal

Ernest Hemingway: *Always willing to lend a helping hand to the one above him.*
F. Scott Fitzgerald

Henry James: *Writes fiction as if it were a painful duty.*
Oscar Wilde

James Joyce: *My God! What a clumsy olla putrida Joyce is! Nothing but old fags and cabbage stumps of quotations from the Bible and the rest, stewed in the juice of deliberate, journalistic dirty-mindedness.*
D. H. Lawrence

John Keats: *His poetry is the* fricasee *of a dead dog.*
Thomas Carlyle

Norman Mailer: *The patron saint of bad journalism.*
Gore Vidal

George Meredith: *As a writer, he has mastered everything except language; as a novelist, he can do everything except tell a story; as an artist, he is everything except articulate.*
Oscar Wilde

Eugene O'Neill: *Basically, an untalented man.*
Truman Capote

Jean-Paul Sartre: *A bag of wind.*
George Orwell

William Shakespeare: *With the single exception of Homer, there is no eminent writer, not even Sir Walter Scott, whom I can despise so entirely as I despise Shakespeare when I measure my mind against his. It would positively be a relief to dig him up and throw stones at him.*
George Bernard Shaw

Gore Vidal: *I've had to smell your works from time to time, and that has helped me to become an expert on intellectual pollution.*
Norman Mailer

Emile Zola: *Zola is determined to show that, if he has not genius, he can at least be dull. And how well he succeeds!*
Oscar Wilde

So what is the new snobbery? It is not only being seen with important names from the world of the arts, politics, journalism and society; it is the pursuit of the obscure and implausible as a *cachet*, in the hope others will be green with envy.

It is lunches at the Savoy Grill and Tate Galley; living in a converted barn; first nights in Theatreland; art gallery press previews; gyroscopic calculators; being able to pronounce at a film club on the flash three frames before the break in a Fellini film; dinner with Leonard Bernstein; decor by David Mlinaric; owning a Noel Coward painting.

Fashion and Shopping Snobbery

*I am not a fashion designer. I am an artist who
works in fashion, an engineer of colour and
form.*
Italian-born US designer Giorgio di Sant'Angelo

It is not a platinum American Express card or a Scottish estate
which truly says more about you than money ever can. When it
comes to truly demonstrable, up-to-the minute snob value, it is
labels which maketh man (or woman).

Nowhere is the new snobbery more instantly applied than in the
world of shopping and fashion. And fortunately at the moment,
London leads the world.

When, in June 1988, the Paris magazine *Elle* sought to define *Les
Nouveaux Snobismes* (literally, the New Snobbery) it was English
style which dominated. That certain *je ne sais quoi* was said to be
rather, that London don't-know-quite-what with a few choice
Franglais phrases like *le sportswear* to denote the best in up-market
clothes.

Chic Paris women were advised to seek the designs of British-
Turkish designer Rifat Ozbek. If this proved a problem, advised
Elle, it was quite acceptable to pop into Marks and Spencer's or
Aquascutum (Paris branch only). *Très chic*, it pointed out, was a
pique-nique in the grand English manner, à la Glyndebourne, with
all the men in – yes – *les smokings* (dinner jackets). During the meal
the game was to play *le christian-name dropping*, e.g. "As I was
saying to Diana the other day . . ."

---

*I mustn't go on singling out names . . . One
must not be a name-dropper, as Her Majesty
remarked to me yesterday . . .*
Norman St John Stevas, now Lord St John of
Fawsley, quoted by Peterborough, *Daily Telegraph*

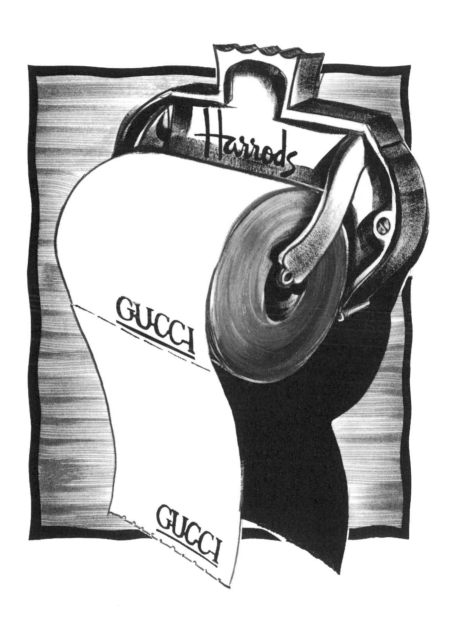

The official name for this English-orientated in-crowd in Paris is BCBG (*bon chic, bon genre*) and *Elle* made one further recommendation for the new French snobbery: English shoes. If you couldn't get your hands on the ultimate dream of Church's shoes, advised the magazine, there were always shoelaces from Lobb of St James's, Prince Charles's shoemakers, to put into your old Hermès foot-cladding.

Shopping in London, of course, requires something like "the knowledge" practised until perfect by *les taxi drivers* and aspirant new snobs should be familiar with the entrances to Harrods, Liberty of Regent Street and Harvey Nichols. They must also memorise the names of the more important shops along New Bond Street (Asprey's and Gucci side only), Jermyn Street, South Molton Street (notably Browns), the King's Road, and Beauchamp Place.

A familiarity with *Vogue, Elle, Vanity Fair, Tatler, Harpers & Queen* (women) and the *Face* (men) is essential for erudite recognition of the following masters and mistresses of the art of fashion:

For Women: Azzedine Alaia, Jean Paul Gaultier, Ralph Lauren, Karl Lagerfeld (Chanel), Yves St Laurent, Bruce Oldfield, Jasper Conran and (the magician himself) Rifat Ozbeck – all clothes; Manolo Blahnik, Maud Frizon – shoes; Edina Ronay – knitwear; Janet Reger – underwear.

For Men: Jasper Conran, Ralph Lauren, Romeo Gigli, Giorgio Armani – clothes; Tommy Nutter – suits; John Lobb – shoes.

Four Giveaway Snobs' Dreams

1 Having a servant to wax your jacket
2 Owning a Jon Bannenberg rubber dinghy
3 Having an Asprey's personal organiser
4 Having your own jet fly to Cuba to stock up with cigars

Of course it is true that many of the names working for Condé Nast recently (*Tatler, Vogue* and *Vanity Fair* etc.) have lived the lives they write about. According to the *Evening Standard*, to get a job there you need to be "thirsty, flirty, and under 30" and preferably with a private income. ("You must also be prepared to work long hours for small change.") Thus recent employees ("the list reads like Debrett's") include the Honourable Louisa Young, Lady Sarah Gordon-Lennox, and Lady Liza Campbell.

It is encouraging to learn that a world of apparent snobbery has real snobbery at its very bosom: it was always so. The founder of *Vogue* in America, Mrs Edna Chase, insisted her girls wore hats, white gloves, and silk stockings at all times. When she hired an editor for the British clone, Alison Settle, Ms Settle was ordered never to take a bus, and to move from Hampstead because it had "no class at all" to a flat with a uniformed porter on the ground floor.

So I moved to a dreary flat in Upper Berkeley Street. That was "class" until Edna came over and discovered there wasn't a uniformed porter on the ground floor. She said: "That's not good enough, Alison." So I had to move again.

You can tell he's got no style if he wears:

grey shoes
brown suits
clip on braces
a digital watch
V-neck sweaters
monogrammed shirts
belt-loop trousers without a belt
plain ties
black polo-neck sweaters
sleeveless T-shirts
ankle socks
and carries a collapsible umbrella

That pales beside the case of the American editor who tried to commit suicide by throwing herself under a subway train.

"We at Vogue *don't throw ourselves under subway trains, my dear,"* Mrs Chase told her. *"If we must, we take sleeping pills."*

Going back to those famous London stores, of course, it must be said that having the requisite will and cash, knowing the intimate geography of Knightsbridge and recognising a Jasper Conran from a Mr Harry may not be enough to help you on the road to setting the Zanzibar aflame with envy of your latest kit.

You have one final obstacle to overcome: another leader on the world snob circuit: *the shop assistant.* One slight tremor on your way through the door as you eye the hiply hip-shaking young things in their latest designer gear – plus their dragon-like superiors hovering on the sidelines like demented spiders – may be enough to condemn you as a no-hoper. Thus you receive either the condescending brush-off – or worse, the full-frontal approach with the hint of being summarily frog-marched off the premises. You know, the one that begins: "Can I help you . . . ?"

Our advice: select two from the following list, and use them in tandem:

1 look them straight in the eye and be condescending first;
2 hire a man in uniform and pretend he's your chaffeur/bodyguard;
3 tread forcefully on their toes;
4 put on an American accent;
5 get your bank manager to ring the shop with a message to expect a favoured client.

> *Now that Vuitton have opened in London's*
> *Bond Street it makes it much easier to acquire*
> *their extensive range without the added cost of*
> *flying to Paris and having to wait in line behind*
> *all those rich orientals.*
> Viviane Ventura, *Guide to Social Climbing*

Well, fine, you have had all the basic theory. Now it's time for the practice. Remember, the new snob's wardrobe should contain such basic minimum items as follows:

Women

Burberry coat
Chanel suit
Bruce Oldfield ballgown
Rifat Ozbek cocktail dress
Yves St Laurent or Christian Lacroix winter outfit
Ralph Lauren jacket
Barbour jacket
Ballantyne cashmere cardigan
Chanel silk blouse
Manolo Blahnik or Maud Frizon shoes
Gucci loafers
Chanel belt
La Perla underwear
Fergal or Bruce Oldfield stockings/tights
Hermès handbag
Hermès silk scarf
Porsche watch

> *Look at this, Jilly dear. It's very me, very Hong Kong . . .*
> Lady in Monsoon clothes shop, Richmond, overheard by *Evening Standard*

Men

Burberry coat
Jasper Conran suit
Armani jacket
Barbour jacket
Levis 501 or Liberto jeans

Chanel or Gucci belt
Liberty ties
Lobb shoes
Rolex Oyster watch
Porsche sunglasses (but only if you can't afford the car)

> *I hoped they would notice that I was sporting a*
> *pair of the finest chinos the Ivy League has to*
> *offer, Royals, white socks and a not unfetching*
> *ice-blue lamb's wool – there's no point*
> *girl-watching if they don't look back.*
> 'Tony Ross', Robert Elms in *In Search of the Crack*

So what is the new snobbery? It's being organised, totally in charge of your life, whilst appearing shambolic, unpushy, cool. Try the Robert Elms trick of a designer crack chiselled into your wall if your place looks too pristine, smooth. Or spurn the High Street, shop at car boot and jumble sales. Arch fogey, A. N. Wilson, is said to "almost live" at his local second hand shop, Pom Pom:

New clothes are so expensive and I wouldn't be seen dead in the ones I could afford. I mean you can go to C & A, but personally I wouldn't.

No new snob would buy anything from a chain store.

Oh but I promise you I do sometimes look scruffy – I often get up and just pull on a floppy sweater and some Jasper Conran trousers.
Gayle Hunnicut, *Today*

Food and Wine Snobbery

So much is the blind Folly of this Age, that the
English Upper classes would rather be imposed
upon by a French Booby than give
Encouragement to a good English cook.
Hannah Glasse, 1769, quoted by Theodore Zeldin,
The French

As the culture of the young-with-money-without-children has
mushroomed, so has the cultural competitiveness which leads to
leisure industry snobbery. And nowhere is this more apparent
than in the world of eating out and eating in – food and wine.

We ought to start with a few hints for the uninitiated. Brill is a
particularly up-market fish, not something to be exclaimed after a
happy meal. Michelin stars do not denote the pressure of your car
tyres – they are a coveted award to only the best restaurants. The
Roux brothers are top restaurateurs and chefs, not musical hall
change-dressers who sing "On Mother Kelly's Doorstep". Hilary
Rubinstein is a man. There are other chefs in London besides
Anton Mosimann though reading the glossy magazines you may
not believe it.

It is easy to become a food or wine snob, without necessarily
great outlay. One of the publishing successes of recent years was a
slim but riveting little volume called, we believe, *The Bluffer's
Guide to Wine*. Other than this, all that is needed to become a
"grapie" is to learn a list of gushing adjectives: "mellifluous",
"luminous", "volcanic", plus a lot of obscure ones the taste of
which no one has even found out, but sound clever when applied
to the vino: E.g., "gossamer-like", "tang of asphalt", "gaberdine-
flavoured".

Life is too short to drink bad wine.
Robin Young, wine editor, *Taste* magazine

Of course, food itself is something you should bone up on. A crash course in the French nomenclature for all kinds of offal would be an ideal starting point (offal has more snob value than real meat, in a typical reversal of reality). Food fads are very "in" – such as refusing any meal that does not come with a spinach side-salad or refusing to eat quails' eggs that are not free range. (Do not, however, make the mistake of saying the same about sturgeons' eggs).

The golden rules of eating out are:

1 Always try to go to a restaurant in its first week; this might be risky but (a) the staff will remember you and (b) if anyone waxes lyrical about your favourite restaurant you have the chance to jump in and say: "Ah, but have you been to . . . ?"

2 Only go where you can see and be seen.

You see more famous faces at lunchtime at the Savoy than anywhere else – Caris Davis, *Evening Standard*.

3 Memorise the names of the head waiter, the chef, the barman, etc. to recount their acquaintance later to your friends.

4 Tip well, but don't get tipsy.

5 Guard your handbag, and watch your umbrella.

★   ★   ★

Wine snobbery has of course a longer pedigree, dare we say vintage, than the new competitiveness of foodies swapping their experiences of the latest cooking fad.

"Amusing, if not distinguished." "A modest little wine." "A little obvious I feel." According to restaurateur Nick Clarke, the perfect put-down to a wine snob is to say: "Have you ever drunk wine from a Japanese virgin's navel?" That is the one experience they are unlikely to recall as, "a rather presumptuous bouquet, I think".

> *I was in a dilemma a couple of years ago when my friend Baron Philippe de Rothschild was coming for dinner . . . What wine do you serve?*
> David Shilling, *Thinking Rich*

Peterborough in the *Daily Telegraph* asked readers to submit the most pompous descriptions they had read of the partaking of the humble grape. This one was a winner:

The name Comte de Vogue is supreme sovereign in the group of the world's red wines. When the wines of '71 produced by these vineyards have attained ten years of age, they will no longer be mere wines, but dreams, liquid grace, elixirs of the gods that one guards like jewels, and preferably drinks only at one's own funeral, for no moment of life can be so precious as to demand such a celebration.

Why do I drink champagne for breakfast?
Doesn't everyone?
Noel Coward

Our advice is to find a reputable wine merchant, (even the man in the off-licence!) seek his advice, and for ever boast of your relationship with your shipper. Anything else is surely being amusing rather than distinguished; and a little presumptuous, what?

"Yeah, I sell quite a few bottles of that Day-oh,
I was sent up to London to learn about it for a
couple of days." Evidently, in that couple of
days, no one had taught the manager of this
particular Hampshire off-licence branch that
Dão is actually pronounced "Downg" . . . And
for those of you who really want to know what
red Vinho Verde tastes like, call A.B. on ABC
1234 . . . But be sure to lay in a stock of
suckling pig too.
Robert Joseph, *Sunday Telegraph*

Lastly, two cautionary tales for foodies and grapies. The grapies bat first in this modern parable from the pen of Garth Gibbs of the *Daily Mirror*.

Mr Gibbs discovered during his holiday that an Australian journalist and television personality had a holiday home in the beautiful countryside of Tuscany. He was remembered for little else but this:

> *One evening he was entertaining friends on his porch. As they lifted their glasses, one of the guests inquired: "Where does this wine come from?"*
>
> *The man from Oz waved towards some vineyards and said proudly: "There . . . from the bottom of my garden."*
>
> *"Doesn't travel very well, does it?" said the guest.*

And the foodies? We loved the tale told in *Harpers and Queen* in April, 1988, of the sojourn to Paris by Mark Birley, doyen of the London clubs, owner of Annabel's, Harry's Bar, etc. and a group of friends.

Nina Campbell told how they had stopped for lunch at a restaurant called Le Trente Trois in the rue de l'Université; "a fairly awful little place with a big black waiter who drained the wine from people's glasses as they left the restaurant.

"Mark thought, 'Wouldn't it be nice to tell Madame 'D' (a New York socialite), who we were seeing that evening, that la toute Paris was there, and that was the latest place."

So, according to Ms Campbell, Mr Birley not only told Madame "D" all about it, but told her to be sure to ask for the house speciality *la tête de nègre*. Madame "D"' allegedly replied: "That's just wonderful. I haven't had a *tête de nègre* since my childhood in San Francisco."

I have only been awarded one star once in my career, that in the lacklustre Egon Ronay's Guide . . .
Alastair Little, of the Soho restaurant of the same name, *Evening Standard*

So what is the new snobbery? It's boycotting food not for politics, but for its cholesterol, fibre, fat, listeria content; it's pouring scorn on Keith Floyd and taking Frank Bruno with HP sauce. It's rejecting nouvelle and Cajun cooking for good English favourites like game pie, tripe, steak and kidney pud. It's letting the farmyard mud dry on your Barbours, and getting health food for the dog.

It's drinking wines (noisily) from the most unexpected places. "Nobody who is anybody could possibly stick with *French* Sauvignon, my God." If you're bored with obscure New Zealand Chardonnays and flattened by white Zinfadels, find Vino Nobile di Montepulciano extremely bohemian and wouldn't wash out your mouth with Krug Grande Cuvée, you have probably made the grade. The trick is to find a wine you like, and spurn the rest. Otherwise make sure to swot up on your *Bluffer's Guide*.

> *Even caviare's perfectly fine if properly served*
> *and not done to impress.*
> Lady Elizabeth Anson of "Party Planners", quoted
> by the *Daily Express*

Home and Property Snobbery

By the way – have you sold your castle yet?
Remark overheard by a friend of the authors

Quite apart from accent, clothes, and *deportment*, perhaps the greatest indicator of whether one has "made it" or not is one's home address. Thus the new snob will make every effort to ensure he or she lives in an acceptable postal district – in a property no matter how *bijou*.

Estates agents trade on it, of course. The lowlier parts of Tufnell Park and West Hampstead will thus become Hampstead/Highgate borders. Meanwhile down-market areas will become transformed to the upwardly mobile with a simple trick of pronunciation: Cla'am for Clapham, St Ockwell for Stockwell. A writer in the *Independent* firmly maintained in September, 1988, he had heard somebody boast of living in Crickle-bois.

The definitive treatment of address snobbery we read came in the *Daily Mail* on July 12, 1930, from literary luminary Evelyn Waugh, who had just moved into St James's Square. This is what he told acquaintances, tradesmen, storepeople and the like; what he did not mention was that this was St James's Square, Holland Park, not the one near Buckingham Palace.

> *Since I have been living here I have realised the importance which two-thirds of the inhabitants of London attach to what they consider "a good address". Again and again lately I have had to give instructions to shops, "Will you send it please to St James's Square . . ."*
>
> *"Very good, sir," the salesman has been all attention and deference.*
> *"Holland Park?" I add.*
> *"Oh!" The change of attitude is instantaneous. "I must inquire whether our van is delivering there this afternoon."*

Of course, one would like to marry a duke's son. One then gets a nice house thrown in.
Honourable Josephine Keys, quoted in the *Daily Mirror*, May 1983

An extrapolation of Mr Waugh's analysis takes us to the conclusion that it is perfectly feasible to have "a good address" without it necessarily having to be in Belgravia, Mayfair or Kensington. Thus there is an Eaton Square in Belgravia; but there is also one in Stanmore. You can choose for yourself a Park Lane but not necessarily in Mayfair. There are three others in Croydon, Edmonton, and Hornchurch. If you go far out east to Forest Gate (perhaps we should call it West Ham borders) you can find a perfectly acceptable address such as Bow Street or Bond Street – both conveniently round the corner from the real life Albert Square.

This is mischief, of course. The obvious tack for the snob without mega-money is to spot the next up-and-coming area and to get in there first. Prices in SW7 are monstrous, but SW5, on the way there we are assured by all the up-market magazines, will soon be cleared of short-stay Australian bedsits to become the new Sloane home on the range.

This reminds us of the gentleman who had a heart attack in a street in those parts. Dying as he undoubtedly was, the pain of cardiac arrest was nothing to the agony he felt when he realised he was in Earl's Court. He mustered enough strength to stagger across the border to South Kensington, with the famous last words:

"I wasn't going to die in SW5."

The borders is a very feudal area really. I mean it is perfectly normal to bump into a belted earl in the Co-op, or a duke in the Post Office. In fact, this will make you laugh. I went into a tiny hairdresser in St Boswell's one morning and I was under the drier with two duchesses, a countess and a marchioness.

Moira Leggat, The Scotsman, quoted by "Pseuds Corner", *Private Eye*

And we recall two other such stories: first of the acquaintance who informed us that he had contracted an *absolutely awful* dose of flu.

"*But don't worry. It's Chelsea flu,*" he confided adding: "*At least I caught it in a nice area.*"

Secondly, the *Daily Telegraph* was able to point out a surprising touch of snobbery in arch-socialist Aneurin Bevan, who in a speech in 1956 in Shoreditch fumed at the undesirability of people of various income groups living in different localities:

> It leads to all kinds of iniquitous social by-products, to intellectual sterilisation, and the most shocking kind of snobbery, and to profound social ignorance . . . Fellows with rolled-up umbrellas should live in the same place as chaps wearing caps . . .

The newspaper went on to remind readers of Mr Bevan's London address: 23 Cliveden Place, SW1 – just round the corner from Eaton Square.

These days though, it is perhaps not quite enough to live at a good address; one has to make sure one's castle has a decent interior as well, which is why for the smart homemaker the names Colefax and Fowler, David Mlinaric, and David Hicks will drop leisurely from the tongue.

According to Anne-Elisabeth Moutet, French correspondent of *Elle* in *Courvoisier's Book of the Best*:

> A house should have an indoors and outdoors swimming pool, private Jacuzzis in every bathroom, a dish antenna to catch every possible TV station direct from the satellite, a gym with a Nautilus machine, a screening room with Dolby equipment, central heating (how can the English survive in those glacial piles?) a helicopter pad, the perfect couple of servants/caretakers to see that everything runs smoothly, and, most essential, his and hers bathrooms.

As for the nouveau riche, *they have no feeling for historic and beautiful buildings.*
Duke of Rutland, *Daily Express*

69

There is not much, naturally, we can add to that, save to say our favourite lines in an estate agent's blurb were these from *Avenue* magazine, New York:

The use of marble in the kitchen is an understatement of the quality inherent in the apartment and not there for mere show or gloss,

and:

A small gymnasium/office, a wine-cooling room, eat-in kitchen with green marble floors and countertops. Central gallery is well suited for showing art collection.

The only caveat we would make to these absolute home essentials is that the superior person should avoid at all costs: flock wallpaper in rooms under 100×30 feet; floral lampshades; kidney-shaped coffee tables; candelabra; and plaster of Paris busts of Johann Sebastian Bach, Julian Lennon, Jayne Mansfield, and Samantha Fox.

Naturally in all the above we have just been talking of London and New York because everything so far has naturally just been about one's *pied à terre* (what the famed hostess Mrs Greville amusingly used to call her *ventre à terre*).

We are of course assuming that you will have a country place too, say a nice little Adam pile, with perhaps a cottage in Normandy or Connecticut, or a villa in Tuscany for the odd weekend thrown in. Unless you were a friend of the late Russell Harty, who seemed to beget a whole show business community among the cottages of Giggleswick, your country abode will be in either Royal Gloucestershire (Charles, Michael, Anne country) or the better parts of Northamptonshire and Leicestershire. At a pinch you could get away with living near Oxford, Winchester, or

---

Actually, residentially speaking, our nearest neighbours are Charles and Di.
Overheard at Kew by the *Evening Standard*

Salisbury; but if anyone mentions "the lawn" at Paddington please remember it does not consist of grass, nor is it the place for picnics or walking the dog: it is a tarmacadamed meeting area where one bumps into people of similar *station*.

The new snob will be well aware that unfashionable places in the provinces all, for some reason, begin with the letter C (Corby, Consett, Castleford) or H (Huddersfield, Halifax), as in the Princess of Wales's horror when she was told of a visit to Humberside:

"What do you think is happening to us tonight? We've got to go to Hull." (Propping one eye open with her fingers) *"It's going to be matchstick time for us."*

> *But how can he buy a dog? He hasn't got a park to exercise it in.*
> Lord Sackville West, owner of Knole Castle, Kent

And, if you have the right kind of property you mustn't forget the staff . . .

I do think servants should not be ill, we have quite enough illness ourselves without their adding to the symptoms.
Lady Diana Cooper

Domestic staff, chauffeurs, and perhaps the only growing breed – the nanny – have long provided upper- and middle-class Britain with its finest excuse for proving class superiority to the less privileged. True, we are no longer in the late nineteenth century when one third of the active female population was engaged in service; and the gentleman's gentleman of today is likely to be far more snobbish than his master (witness the character in the Marc cartoon of 1976: *I don't believe in class differences, but fortunately my butler disagrees with me.*)

If you haven't already got a nanny – get one. All the best couples do, many of them with children. If the best you can do is to secure

71

the service of a cleaning woman and gardener/handyman, you will know to refer to them as your manservant and maid (not respectively).

In the past, of course, servants were not treated with condescension so much as with contempt. Margaret Powell, who chronicled her life below stairs in a series of best-selling books, recalled how she had gone to the Opera with her husband and was greeted by an elderly lady with a patronising boom:

"Are you not Margaret Langley who was my cook when I lived in London?"

On another occasion she asked her employer if she could possibly borrow a book from the library, to be met with the cruel squelch:

"Of course you may, Margaret. But I didn't know you could read."

*   *   *

Servants were always expected to know their place. The matter of Labour MP Mr Ron Brown, and what he may or may not have done in a Commons washroom, led Joe Haines in the *Daily Mirror* to recall an earlier potential scandal when a Conservative MP and a waitress were found in an indecent pose in a Commons committee room.

Those days were more decorous. The affair was hushed up. And the House authorities did the only decent and dignified thing they could think of.

They sacked the waitress.

*   *   *

To some, of course, life without servants would be intolerable. In 1941 Jock, later Sir John Colville, assistant private secretary to Sir Winston Churchill for much of the war, persuaded the great man to let him join the RAF. Sir John told in his memoirs, *Action This Day*, how Churchill was horrified to hear that he would be starting as an aircraftsman, 2nd class.

"You must not do that," Churchill insisted. *"You won't be able to take your man."*

*   *   *

The indelible picture of P. G. Wodehouse's Jeeves is of a manservant far more acute in the ways of the world, more intelligent, even, than his employer, with a talent for subtle and snobbish humour. Reality may not disabuse us of this notion.

This experience of a reader of the *Sunday Telegraph*, recalled in a letter to the paper in 1981, is no doubt typical:

When I went up to change for dinner, I found that the butler had unpacked my clothes, but that some of them were missing. When I mentioned this to my hostess, she said: "Oh! Bates thought that some of them were unsuitable and threw them away."

* * *

So what is the new snobbery? It's renting, not buying, as saith asthmatic author Andy Hislop:

It is quite liberating. It means you avoid having those ghastly conversations about how much your property is worth.

If you rent from the Duke of Westminster, say a little place in Eaton Square, it might be quite nice too . . .

If you're buying a house for 150 grand you don't want to be shown round by Joe Bloggs of Oik and Oik.

Winkworth spokesman quoted by Tina Brown,
Life as a Party

Travel Snobbery

*We are staying with Sheikh Yamani, who came
out to Mustique this year. Don't ask me what
one does in Saudi Arabia. We will have to find
out.*

Honourable Colin Tennant

In the great squash game of life which is the new snobbery, no
single pursuit demands more attention than being well travelled –
exceedingly well travelled, in fact. The competition is in the realms
of flame-throwers at dawn; at a recent cocktail party before we
Joneses could even manage a "how do you do?" we had been told
in an opening sentence that another couple had recently been in
Hong Kong, Hollywood, and Bali. We also award five gold
upturned noses to the top Merrill Lynch executive who gave
Who's Who as his interests "collecting Michelin Guide stars and
airline boarding passes".

Yes, travel snobbery is really a "collecting" hobby, except that
one is collecting the names of hotels, restaurants, swimming pools
etc. in obscure and romantic outposts rather than stamps, the
sightings of rare birds or locomotive numbers.

The game has become so frenzied, however, that a certain
amount of stocktaking is vital. It is possible to book outwardly
exotic looking hotels in top snob spots only to find them in-
habited by men in medallions and gold bracelets and women
drinking half pints of Malibu. The Seychelles sounds a romantic

---

*– My son's just gone to Istanbul. I don't know
whether he'll avoid the vice. But he's staying
with a middle-class family.
– Oh, that's far worse.*
Quoted by Roy Perrot, *The Aristocrats*

75

enough place but its present naffness was well summed up by Rebecca Willis in *Vogue*:

> *A friend was so embarrassed to be married after a twelve-hour flight crammed with billing and cooing newly weds, that she could hardly speak to her new husband on arrival in paradise. Worse still, there was a constant flow of British couples getting married by the pool, with the duty manager acting as best man.*

The important thing to remember is that it is not just good enough to arrive at the right place. You must be in the right place at the right time. Just as you would not turn up at Mégève carrying skis in August, you must hit New Orleans (for the Mardi Gras) in February, the Caribbean in January, Cannes in July, and Rajasthan in November (for the Pushkar Camel Fair).

Apart from that, can we offer these helpful tricks of the trade to the would-be travel snob?

1 YOU DON'T need to have travelled all over the world to have a truly impressive passport. For the price of a few pounds, you can fill it up with visas to interesting destinations like, say, the People's Democratic Republic of the Yemen. Write to a few embassies and consulates for the forms.

2 PRISTINE LUGGAGE is a complete giveaway. Until the authors open their planned batter-your-suitcase-like-they-do-at-Terminal 3-until-it-looks-authentic service, we suggest four drops onto hard concrete from a height of three feet, then a glancing blow bottom right from either a machete or cut-throat razor.

3 ALWAYS SWOT UP on where you are going, reading all the travel books you can find in the local library. Make a list of the top glitz hotels and restaurants. Then visit them, one by one. You may only need the outlay of a drink in each; but you have *been*.

Once you've checked your suitcase in (early, please, if its tacky . . .)
Viviane Ventura *Guide to Social Climbing*

4 COLLECT EVERYTHING – that means when you are in the expensive hotel bar (*see* 3) you will pick up the courtesy pack of matches; on the airline you will pick up the logoed magazines, sugar packets, pens etc., all to leave about your home to faze your friends.

In addition to knowing 'must' summer locations – Monte Carlo, Marbella, Martha's Vineyard – the well-versed traveller will have a working knowledge of at least five ski resorts. These will naturally have included Val d'Isère if not Klosters or Gstaad. Do not admit any knowledge of Verbier (cramped, noisy, common).

For really making an impression, however, a skiing trip to North America is vital. Aspen has been losing out to Vail as far as Colorado goes (Gerry Ford, Jimmy Connors, Alan Bond live there in winter). A flirtation with Sun Valley, Idaho, however, suggests skiing skills beyond normal reach. It could be your ambition to go instead to the Hotel Portillo, Portillo, Chile, but that might just sound a trifle *Acapulco* for some.

A little matter of etiquette abroad can be summed up like this. Although a duke's accent will take precedence over an earl's accent, any English accent takes precedence over any other. The Englishman travels on no other basis.

In Douglas Sutherland's excellent *The English Gentleman Abroad* the Duke of St Albans tells the story of how, in Arizona, he was asked what kind of accent he possessed.

I pointed out that it was she and not I who had an accent, his grace writes.

Oh – I guess you must be an Australian, was the reply.

> *What a beautiful morning it's been out on deck*
> *. . . Only on the third-class tourist passengers'*
> *deck was it a sultry overcast dull morning, but if*
> *you do things on the cheap you must expect*
> *these things.*
> Spike Milligan, *A Dustbin of Milligan*

One of the ways of seeing the world is of course through third parties. You know the sort of thing: "I'm Jeremy's second cousin from Gloucester, he's told me to get in touch because *it just so happens* I'm going to be in your neck of the woods . . ." There is no sleight of network connection of course that the well versed travel snob will not pull to secure luxury accommodation and subsidised meals in grand surroundings. Pledges to write letters of introduction must be sought ruthlessly at dinner and cocktail parties. Contacts abroad must be prised from colleagues and friends with the skill of a surgeon. Then phone calls to the generous host or hostess must leave no room for manoeuvre: "Yes, I said 8.40 your time at the airport . . . Sorry, I can't hear you . . . line's gone a bit crackly . . . 8.40 at the airport . . . can't hear you . . . see you in the arrivals hall, then."

To avoid embarrassing and costly reciprocity, the host and hostess should not be 100 per cent English or American. If they are authentic, first generation ex-pats, (or Americans) of course, a return invitation must be offered. If your hosts are Antipodean, South African, new Commonwealth, or otherwise not automatically eligible for golf club membership, it is perfectly acceptable to tear up and forget any postcard or telegram which arrives saying "Remember your stay in Florence – I am coming your country – Arrive Heathrow 16.00 Thurs . . . Please meet me . . ." The true travel snob would never get mixed up with foreign *tourists*.

Having tried this [ordering a wheelchair at the airport] I can attest that for speed, comfort and efficiency, there's nothing like it. You sit, an emperor in your palanquin, ploughing through the peasantry, scattering them to right and left . . .
Jessica Mitford, *Mail and Femail*

So what is the new snobbery? It's going to a country house week-end and being careful not to remark on the Rubens and Van Dycks. It's ringing up a hotel with the imperious request: "Do you have a helicopter landing facility?"

There are two classes of travel: first class, and with children.
Robert Benchley

Sporting Snobbery

There is one major field of human endeavour where the true snob can prove he or she is definitely of a privileged elite and not one of the oiks: that of sport. And, fortunately, it is not necessary to be a participant – nay, not even an *aficionado* – so much as possessing the nimble footwork to give of one's best from the pavilion, grandstand, track, ring or riverside.

The gentlemen *v* players division much allied in our class conciousness with the game of cricket in fact pervades all the sporting activities with which the truly aloof wishes to be associated.

These can be roughly summed up as (a) anything to do with horses, especially hunting; (b) anything to do with horses, especially polo; (c) anything to do with horses, especially racing; and (d) games played at every major or minor public school (e.g. cricket, fives, rowing, bullying, raiding the tuck shop, swiping one's neighbour's ruler, etc. etc.).

In the latter category it should be remarked what a fine example in later life the ex-public schoolboys of the Rugby Football Union set in the defence of all snobbery's guiding principles. Woe betide the rugger man, no matter how impoverished, who sells his soul to play the dreaded cloth-cap Rugby League (even as an amateur). No fate – excommunication, a life ban, ritual disembowelment, being forced to watch a year's back episodes of *A Question of Sport*, is good enough for such a bounder.

Back in the 1940s, Welsh R. U. international George Parsons was denied the honour of his cap merely for letting drop the word "league" while talking on unemployment. It took thirty years before he was finally awarded his pardon – and his cap – in 1977.

England needs to pull itself together. As I drove to Ascot the other day, I noticed workmen by the roadside leaning on their spades doing nothing at all. Did they not realise the damage this kind of behaviour does to our country?
Queen, 1946

So what are the requirements for becoming a sporting snob? Well, little else but (a) an ability to ride a horse; (b) membership of a good polo, yacht, golf, cricket or tennis club; (c) an aptitude to learn the peculiar vocabularies implicit in top-class sports; and (d) total obliviousness, when decked out in the peculiar uniforms, ties, caps, badges and colours of your chosen sporting troop, to the fact that to your fellow man you look quite ridiculous.

Don't go to Ascot. (*Pure murder* – Lady Olga Maitland. *A Clacton for social climbers* – Richard Compton Miller). It's now so *frightfully* nouveau riche. Never been the same since Linda Lovelace was allowed in and Princess Diana turned back at the gate.

Sporting events to aim for are: (a) the America's Cup (wherever, whenever); (b) Glorious Goodwood; (c) the Derby at Epsom; (d) the Prix de l'Arc de Triomphe; (e) the Monaco Grand Prix and, of course, Henley. If you can fit in the Second Test at Lord's nobody will mind, but whatever you do, don't take a portable telephone to any of the above, or you might as well have opted to play Rugby League.

★　★　★

There can be few more sniffy institutions than the average golf club. Some try to discriminate fairly by making the cost of joining prohibitive. For example, in February 1989 the new East Sussex golf club priced exclusivity at a lofty £16,000 membership. To join the toppest-notch Los Angeles Country Club will cost you a cool $75,000, that is if you make the top of the membership list before you are round to meet the great scorekeeper in the sky.

It can happen to the illustrious. Ludovic Kennedy was black-balled at Muirfield, and claims he was similarly treated by the Senior Golfers' Society (their version: he was merely unsuccessful in six successive ballots). The "quotas" applied to Jews and the Japanese have led them to the inevitable setting up of their own golf clubs like Dyrham Park and Coombe Hill.

Hollywood mogul, Jack Warner, was declared unacceptable at the exclusive Lakeside club, which led to one Ronald Reagan resigning in protest at his then boss's treatment. Another legendary studio chief, Louis B. Mayer, was famed on the course for having a unique approach. He played with no partner and two caddies. When he hit the ball, one caddy was in position down the fairway to find the ball; the second then sprinted ahead to locate himself for the next shot. Mr Mayer meanwhile puffed up behind to play. You see, the former junk dealer from a small village near Minsk had been told it was classy to play golf; but he never understood that the object of the game was to go round in as few strokes as possible – he thought the idea was to go round in the fastest time. At the end of the round he would check his watch and exclaim: "We made it in an hour and seven minutes! Three minutes better than yesterday!"

Two other favourite items of golf snobbery: when South Korean strongman General Chun first came to power as president, he had the unique distinction of being prevented from playing on a golf course in his own country. It was a US army course, the weapons of his bodyguards were ruled "out of order" and he was blackballed.

And then there was the case of the woman pilot who had to make a forced landing between the seventeenth and eighteenth holes of the exclusive Burning Tree club in Washington, in 1983. The members knew exactly how to handle such an emergency. Quoting rule 3 (b) (no women on the premises) they quickly summoned a cab and sent her on her way.

If there is an annual event, of course, which allows us to preserve the old amateur sporting values, look down our noses at the artisans, and avoid the worst of so-called "corporate hospitality"*, that occasion is Henley, where at times it may be difficult to remember that rowing also takes place during the week. One debutante is fondly remembered for arriving at the gate of the Stewards' Enclosure and exclaiming in the loudest of voices: "Daphne! You never said Henley was on the *rivah*!"

The symbol of the Leander Club is of course the hippopotamus and it is said that the hippo and the Leander man are the only two animals to have their noses *perpetually* in the air. It is some of these pink gin and Pimm's–imbibing beasties from their pink palace lair who have done much to hold the line for upper-middle class civilisation up to 1938, managing to keep those occupied in menial tasks from soiling the reputation of oarsmanship, and more recently, fighting against the admission of women.

*Kept to the West side of the river, or well downstream from the Stewards' Enclosure.

You must admire the attempts to keep the lager louts at bay.

In 1970 an application for the opening of a fish and chip shop in Henley's main street was turned down by town councillors on the grounds that "it is felt that a fish and chip shop is not appropriate for a place like this." How nice if all the nation's planners had the same farsightedness and fortitude. (The authors believe there would be no violence late at night if all young people were merely compelled to drink only Pimm's).

Michael Parkinson tells the story of how, as a young reporter, he tried to unravel Henley's mysteries.

> *I turned up outside the Stewards' Enclosure, where I was confronted by a man wearing a school cap with an oversized peak. All I could see was the neb of his cap as he studied a clipboard.*
>
> *I announced my name, occupation, and intention to write an article explaining Henley to the British public.*
>
> *"Really," said the cap.*
>
> *"So I'd like to ask you a few questions," I said.*
>
> *"Fire away," the neb replied.*
>
> *"Well," I burbled, "Henley is said to be very exclusive. What kind of people don't you want down here?"*
>
> *"People like you," he said with a sigh.*

This explains much about Henley, and its extraordinary fascination for the would-be master or mistress of snobbery. Perhaps it is best summed up by the excellent Peter Coni, the man who has done the most to restore the fortunes of Henley and put it on the world social map:

> *I think it's a psychological thing. You tell 'em they can't get in and they all want to come.*

⋆   ⋆   ⋆

> *Who these days would hire a deer forest or a grouse moor if he were liable at any time to see the hideous apparition of 'Arry in appalling checks on the skyline?*
> W. Bromley Davenport, MP

At the apex of sporting snobbery are of course the so-called "country" pursuits – so-called because you need to own something approaching the size of a country to overcome the expense of taking part. These can be broken down roughly into (a) pursuit of game on horseback; (b) pursuit of game on foot; and (c) pursuit of game in large extended Wellingtons while thigh deep in water.

As to the latter sport, Dr Johnson likened it to "a stick and string with a worm at one end and a fool at the other", though according to the *Tatler* fishing is now "a realm of dead men's shoes so exclusive that the only way to infiltrate your rod is to know the right people".

Before considering whether to inflitrate your rod or not, you might consider three cautionary tales from the same article in the *Tatler*, by Crawford Little:

First, beware of members of the gentry falling on your head. This with reference to the squire who married into the family owning the Oykel, an exclusive and snobbish river. After m'lady died, the squire decided that the world suffered from too many hideous and vulgar apparitions for him to contend with. He ordered that straightway a platform should be built in a tree and that all his meals be served there.

Then there was the fisherwoman who looked up from her midstream position in the River Dee to see the Queen. She curtsied. The waters promptly swept into her waders and she was sunk.

Thirdly, and no more about infiltrating rods, please, there was the poor unfortunate who, casting for the first time on the Dee, caught a lady guest's Italian boyfriend who, the ghillie was quick to notice, was sitting on a deck-chair wearing nothing but a jock-strap. Bystanders looked on astonished as the tanned continental hulk was dragged towards the riverbank.

> *Ian Botham, Phil Edwards and David Gower lowered the tone of the Tweed by buying netting rights on the mouth but were fortunately bought out by the Atlantic Salmon Conservation Trust.*
> Tatler

Nonetheless, as the *Tatler* was quick to point out, there is one great triumph of snobbery possible for the polished, compleat angler. George V was rather adept at it – the propensity for having triumphed over the catch, going on to shoot the fish squarely in the head – "thus combining two hooray activities in one go". Hooray!

Least Tactful Remark During The Shooting Season

We are indebted to the London *Evening Standard* for the story of how, after a pheasant shoot at Sandringham, guests of the Prince and Princess of Wales were just sitting down to a lunch of what appeared to be a particularly unedifying stew. Suddenly in burst one of the young female guests clutching a portable telephone.

"I've just been talking to Tally," she exclaimed, a reference to the Duchess of Westminster, who was hostess at a simultaneous event at Eaton Hall, near Chester.

"For their shooting lunch they're having real *alligator stew,"* the young thing enthusiastically gasped to a stony royal silence.

So what is the new snobbery? It's spurning Ascot for the more restrained 'glorious' Goodwood where it's fashionable *not* to dress up. It's owning your own polo ponies; it's not wearing one item of clothing, down to your scanties, that hasn't been paid for by your sponsor; it's renting a shooting lodge from the Prince of Wales. It's smoking your own salmon; it's being invited to play in a charity match at Lord's. It's being an Oxford *and* Cambridge blue in different sports; it's announcing your own challenge for the America's Cup.

So What Is The New Snobbery?

Basically, it's dropping:
* names, not aitches;
* unsuitable friends, not clangers;
* *in* on people who might be useful to you; and
* little notes of purple prose into the palms of those who can pull you up into their world.

It's having the right address: rent, or buy; owner or occupier; mistress, kept woman, or (superior) squatter.

> *Don't* admit to *South* Chelsea or *West* Hampstead or Salford. Talk up your address. For Birmingham, read Warwickshire; for Warrington, Cheshire, etc.
>
> *Do* broadcast your address to all and sundry, best of all in inch high, super-embossed type on the most elegant of notepaper.

It's knowing the right people:

> *Don't* make up to anyone who hasn't got (a) a title; (b) a private jet or helicopter; (c) a string of racehorses; or (d) a record in the current Top 10.
>
> *Do* make the most of your opportunities by going to memorial services, private viewings at art galleries and first night performances.

It's partying at the right places (and at the right times):

Tim Bell, Mrs Thatcher's advertising guru, was able to dine out on the story that he had spent Boxing Day at Chequers with the Prime Minister. Certainly not, it was *Christmas Day*, he crowed.

> *Don't* wait for the invite to come. Pursue your hosts with Roland Rat-like cunning.
>
> *Do* seek out the right arms, not so much to lean on, but to gatecrash with.

It's having the best super-sophisticated gadgets:

like having one's own desktop super-refracting telescope or

I'm no snob. I have friends from comprehensive schools. It's the Yuppies I can't tolerate.
Penny Montford, deb, ITV's *First Tuesday*

---

cyclotron and linear accelerator, Ayurveda electric bath à la Margaret Thatcher, or Heathrow-style explosives scanner in the hall.

Don't buy anything anyone you know has already got;

Do remember to buy a plug so your latest mega-Dolby-whizz-bang-stereoquadro-F111-nucleo-whatdoyercallit can actually work.

It's wearing the right clothes:

swot up on style. Read the glossies from cover to cover. Go to every fashion event you can.

Don't ever cheapskate with High Street imitations, no matter how many credit cards they offer you;

Do insist on designer labels, right down to your cotton socks.

It's having the right recreations:

Do take up fishing, shooting, yachting or equestrianism.

Don't go greyhound racing (not even in a private box), to darts matches or snooker (not even if you're Steve Davis or the editor of the *Observer*).

It's being exquisitely arty:

Don't say anything predictable at a party – pretend they're all pigeons and you'll soon have them eating out of your hand.

Do seek out long-forgotten authors and composers to drop into conversations like golden pebbles in a pool.

It's travelling to exotic locations:

this is what truly sets apart the modern sophisticate from the knotted handkerchief brigade.

Don't carry new luggage/go from Luton Airport/take your own sandwiches and flask.

Do choose your destinations just for the name (no matter how downbeat the place you're staying in) and seek to join the jetsetters by the pool. If you can't get introduced – spray insect repellent on them. It never fails.

Wales has always had this effect on me: no sooner do I arrive than I'm seized by a panic to escape before some idiot seals off the border and traps me there forever.

Irma Kurtz, *Evening Standard*

But bear these words in mind:

The true snob never rests; there is always a higher goal to attain, and there are by the same token, always more and more people to look down upon.
Russell Lynes, "The New Snobbism", *Harpers* magazine, November 1950

Bibliography

Barrow, Andrew, *The Flesh is Weak*. Hamish Hamilton 1980

Barrow, Andrew, *Gossip 1920–1970*. Hamish Hamilton 1978

Barrow, Andrew, *International Gossip 1970–1980*. Hamish Hamilton 1983

Bedford, John, Duke of, *A Silver Plated Spoon*. Reprint Society 1960

Bence-Jones, Mark, and Montgomery-Massingberd, Hugh, *The British Aristocracy*. Constable 1979

Boller, Paul J. Jnr., *Presidential Wives*. Oxford 1988

Bragg, Richard, *Small Oxford Book of Snobs*. Oxford, 1983

Buckle, Richard (Ed.), *U and non-U Revisited*. Debrett's 1978

Celebrity Research Group, *The Bedside Book of Celebrity Gossip*. Prince Paperbacks, New York 1984

Cooper, Jilly and Hartman, Tom, *Violets and Vinegar*. Allen and Unwin 1980

Egremont, Lord, *Wyndham and Children First*. Macmillan 1968

Eliot, Valerie (Ed), *The Letters of T. S. Eliot, Vol. I*. Faber 1988

Elms, Robert, *In Search of the Crack*. Viking 1988

Fadiman, Clifton (Ed.), *The Little, Brown Book of Anecdotes*. Little, Brown, New York 1985

Glendinning, Victoria, *Vita: The Life of V. Sackville-West*. Weidenfeld 1983

Green, Michael, *The Peterborough Book*. David & Charles 1980

Grobel, Laurence, *Conversations with Capote*. Hutchinson 1985

Hilton, Audrey (Ed.), *This England: Selections from the New Statesman*. Allen & Unwin 1982

Hilton, Audrey (Ed.), *The England 1965–1968: Selections from the New Statesman*. New Statesman 1968

Lacey, Robert, *Aristocrats*. Hutchinson 1983

Lynes, Russell, *Snob*. New York 1953

Mason, Philip, *The English Gentleman*. Constable 1982

Masters, Brian, *Great Hostesses*. Constable 1982

Mortimer, John, *In Character*. Allen Lane 1983

Nicolson, Harold, *Good Behaviour*. Constable 1986

Plowden, Alison, *Lords of the Land*. Michael Joseph 1984

Powell, Margaret, *The Treasure Upstairs*. Peter Davis 1970

Pringle, Margaret, *Dance Little Ladies*. Orbis 1977

Ross, Alan S. C., *How to Pronounce It*. Hamish Hamilton 1970

Shilling, David, *Thinking Rich*. Robson 1986

Sinclair, Andrew, *The Last of the Best*. Weidenfeld 1969

Sutherland, Douglas, *The English Gentleman*. Debrett's 1978

Sutherland, Douglas, *The English Gentleman Abroad*. Burke's Peerage 1984

Sutherland, Douglas, *The English Gentleman's Wife*. Debrett's 1979

Turner, E. S., *Amazing Grace*. Michael Joseph 1975

Ventura, Viviane, *Viviane Ventura's Guide to Social Climbing*. Macmillan 1983

Waugh, Auberon, *The Diaries of Auberon Waugh, 1976–1985: A Turbulent Decade*. Private Eye 1985

Waugh, Auberon, *Four Crowded Years: Diaries 1972–1976*. Private Eye 1976